Preface

Discrete Mathematics is a foundational pillar in computer science and mathematics, providing essential tools and frameworks for logical reasoning, algorithm design, and data structure development. For students pursuing the BCA program at the Indira Gandhi National Open University (IGNOU), mastering this subject is vital for academic and professional success. With this in mind, **"IGNOU BCA Discrete Mathematics Previous Year Unsolved Papers MCS 013"** has been compiled to offer learners a practical and focused approach to exam preparation by engaging them directly with real, unsolved questions from past examinations.

This book serves as more than just a repository of previous year question papers—it is a challenge-driven resource designed to strengthen problem-solving skills and deepen conceptual understanding. The unsolved format encourages independent thinking, critical analysis, and active learning. By working through these carefully selected questions, students can enhance their familiarity with exam patterns, identify key topics, and build the confidence necessary to tackle even the most complex problems in discrete mathematics. We are grateful to the educators and learners whose feedback and insight have helped shape this book, and we hope it becomes a valuable companion in your academic journey.

Table of Contents

MCS - 013

MCA-Revised / BCA-Revised

Chapter 1: Term-End Examination, June- 2014

MCS-013: DISCRETE MATHEMATICS

Time: 2 hours

Maximum Marks: 50

Note: (i). Question number 1 is compulsory.

(ii). Attempt any three questions from the rest.

1. (a) Let $f(x) = 1/x$ and $g(x) = x^3 + 2$ where x € R. Find (f+ g) (x) and (fg) (x)? **3**

(b) Draw Venn diagram to represent A ▲ B where A and B are two sets. **3**

(c) If A and B are two mutually exclusive events such that P(A) = 0.3 and P(B) = 0.4 What is the probability that either A or B does not occur? **2**

(d) Prove that $\frac{1}{2} + \frac{1}{2.3} + ... + \frac{1}{n(n+1)} = \frac{n}{n+1}$ using Mathematical Induction. **3**

(e) Show that p ∨(q ∧ r) and (p∨q)∧(p∨r) are logically equivalent. **3**

(f) Prove that product of two odd integers is an odd integer? **3**

(g) How many different strings can be made from the letters of the word "SUCCESS" using all the letters? **3**

2. (a) Let A =R - {3} and B= R - {1}. f: A ⟶B defined by f (x) = $\frac{x-2}{x-3}$ find f^{-1}? **5**

(b) Let R is the relation on the set of strings of Hindi letters such that a **R**b if f l(a) = l(b) where l(x) is length of string x. Show that R is an equivalence relation. **5**

3. (a) Write contrapositive, converse and the inverse of the implication "The home team does not win whenever it is raining." **3**

(b) Draw the logic circuit for the expression Y=ABC+A' C' + B' C' **4**

(c) Determine the number of integer solutions to the equation $x_1 + x_2 + x_3 + x_4 = 7$, where $x_1 \geq 0$ ∀i=1, 2, 3, 4. **3**

4. (a) Five balls are to be placed in three boxes. Each box can hold all the five balls. In how

Many ways can we place the balls so that no box is empty if balls and boxes are different? **5**

(b) Show that $r \rightarrow s$ can be derived from $p \rightarrow (q \rightarrow s)$, $\sim r \vee p$ and q.

5. (a) Show that a map f:R $\rightarrow$R defined by $f(x) = 2x + 1$ for x€**R** is a objective map from R to R. **4**

(b) If $f = \begin{Bmatrix} 1 & 2 & 3 \\ 2 & 3 & 1 \end{Bmatrix}$ and $g = \begin{Bmatrix} 1 & 2 & 3 \\ 3 & 2 & 1 \end{Bmatrix}$ Find *fog* and *gof*? **4**

(c) List all the permutations of {a, b, c}. **2**

MCS-013

MCA-Revised / BCA-Revised

Chapter 2: Term-End Examination, December- 2014

MCS-013: DISCRETE MATHEMATICS

Time: 2 hours

Maximum Marks: 50

Note: (i). Question number 1 is compulsory.

(ii). Attempt any three questions from the rest.

1. (a) Let A = {a, b, c, d}, B = {1, 2, 3} and R = {(a, 2), (b, 1), (c, 2), (d, 1)}. Is R a function? Why? **3**

(b) Under what conditions on sets A and B, AxB=B x A? Explain. **3**

(c) How many bit strings of length 8 contain at least four 1s? **3**

(d) Show that the proposition p ⟶ q and $\sim p \, v \, q$are logically equivalent? **2**

(e) Use mathematical induction to show that n! ≥ 2^{n-1} for n ≥ 1. **3**

(f) A coin is tossed **n** times. What is the probability of getting exactly **r** heads? **3**

(g) Prove that if x and y are rational numbers, then x + y is rational. **3**

2. (a) Find f -1, where f is defined by f(x) = $x^3 - x$ where x € R. **5**

(b) Let the set A = {1, 2, 3, 4, 5, 61 and R is defined as R = {(i, j) | |i - j| = 2}. Is 'R' transitive? Is 'R' reflexive? Is 'R' symmetric? **5**

3. (a) What are the inverse, converse and contrapositive of the implication "If today is holiday, then I will go for a movie."? **3**

(b) Draw the logic circuit for **Y = AB'C + ABC' + AB'C'** **4**

(c) In how many ways can a prize winner choose three books from a list of 10 bestsellers, if repeats are allowed? **3**

4. (a) What is understood by the logical quantifiers? How would you represent the following

propositions and their negations using logical quantifiers: **5**

(i) There is a lawyer who never tells lies.

(ii) All politicians are not honest.

(b) Show that $(\sim p \wedge (\sim q \wedge r)) \vee (q \wedge r) \vee (p \wedge r) \Leftrightarrow r$ **3**

(c) Define Modus Tollens. **2**

5. (a) If R is the set of all real numbers, then show that a map g: R ⟶ R defined by g(x) = x for x € R is a bijective map. **4**

(b) Let A = {1,2,3,4} and $f = \begin{pmatrix} 1 & 2 & 3 & 4 \\ 2 & 4 & 1 & 3 \end{pmatrix}$ $g = \begin{pmatrix} 1 & 2 & 3 & 4 \\ 4 & 1 & 2 & 3 \end{pmatrix}$ Find *fog* and *gof*. **4**

(c) A club has 25 members. How many ways are there to choose four members of the club to serve on an executive committee? **2**

MCS-013

MCA-Revised / BCA-Revised

Chapter 3: Term-End Examination, June- 2015

MCS-013: DISCRETE MATHEMATICS

Time: 2 hours

Maximum Marks: 50

Note: (i). Question number 1 is compulsory.

(ii). Attempt any three questions from the rest.

1. (a) Write down the truth table of $p \rightarrow q \wedge \sim r \leftrightarrow r \oplus q$ Also explain whether it is a tautology or not. **5**

(b) Show that $\sqrt{5}$ is irrational. **4**

(c) Give the geometric representation of R X {2}. **3**

(d) Find the f inverse of the function f: f(x) = $x^3 - x$ **3**

(e) Present a direct proof of the statement: "Square of an odd integer is odd." **3**

(f) How many permutations are there for the word "UNIVERSITY"? **2**

2. (a) (i) Check whether (A U B) ∩ C = A U (B ∩ C) or not, using Venn Diagram. **3**

(ii) Find the dual of A U (B U C). **2**

(b) Prove that C (n, r) = C (n, n — r), for $0 \leq r \leq n$, n € N **5**

3. (a) State and prove Addition Theorem of Probability. **5**

(b) Show that in any group of 30 people, we can always find 5 people who were born on the same day of the week. **3**

(c) State Pigeonhole principle. Also give an example of its application. **2**

4. (a) What is the probability that a number between 1 and 200 is divisible by neither 2, 3, 5 nor 7? **3**

(b) In how many ways can 20 students be grouped into 3 groups? **3**

(c) In how many ways can r distinct objects be distributed into 6 different boxes with at least two boxes empty? **4**

5. (a) Give an example of a compound proposition that is neither a tautology nor a contradiction. **2**

(b) Show that $2^n > n^3$ for $n \geq 10$. **5**

(c) Draw the logic circuit for the following Boolean expression: **x.y + x. y' + x' . y.** **3**

MCS-013

MCA-Revised / BCA-Revised

Chapter 4: Term-End Examination, December- 2015

MCS-013: DISCRETE MATHEMATICS

Time: 2 hours

Maximum Marks: 50

Note: (i). Question number 1 is compulsory.

(ii). Attempt any three questions from the rest.

1. (a) Write the truth value of the disjunction of "The earth is flat" and "3 + 5 = 2". **2**

(b) If p and q are two propositions, then show that ~ (p V q) ≡ ~ p Λ~ q. **4**

(c) Use Mathematical induction to prove that $1 + \frac{1}{4} + \frac{1}{9} + \ldots\ldots + \frac{1}{n^2} \leq 2 - \frac{1}{n} \forall n \in N$ **4**

(d) If f: R --> R is a function such that f(x) = 3x + 2, prove that f is one-one onto. Also, find the inverse of f. **4**

(e) How many integers between 100 and 999 consist of distinct even digits? **3**

(f) Show that the number of words of length n on an alphabet of m letters is m^n **3**

2. (a) Prove that: $\frac{(n+1)}{(r+1)}$ C(n, r) = C(n + 1, r + 1). **5**

(b) Express the Boolean expression in three variables **(x + y' + z') (xy + x'z)** in DNF. **5**

3. (a) Two dice, one red and one white, are rolled. What is the probability that the white die turns up a smaller number than the red die. **4**

(b) State and explain De Morgan's law for Boolean algebra. Also, explain duality principle with the help of an example. **4**

(c) In how many distinct ways is it possible to seat eight persons at a round table? **2**

4. (a) Use Mathematical induction to prove that $1^2 + 2^2 + 3^2 + \ldots + n^2 = \frac{n(n+1)(2n+1)}{6} \forall n \in N$

(b) Find the Boolean expression C for the following logic circuit: **4**

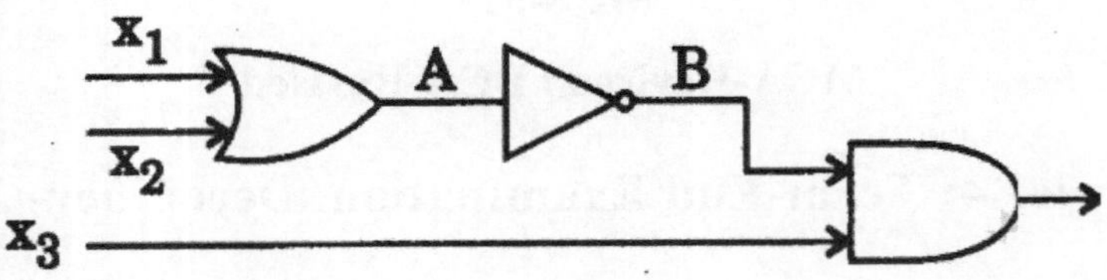

(c) Prove the following equivalence: $\sim \forall x P(x) \equiv \exists x \sim P(x)$ **2**

5. (a) Verify that p ∧ q ∧~ p is a contradiction and $p \rightarrow q \leftrightarrow -pVq$is a tautology. **5**

(b) Show that√2 is irrational. **5**

MCS-013

MCA-Revised / BCA-Revised

Chapter 5: Term-End Examination, June- 2016

MCS-013: DISCRETE MATHEMATICS

Time: 2 hours

Maximum Marks: 50

Note: (i). Question number 1 is compulsory.

(ii). Attempt any three questions from the rest.

1. (a) Using the principle of mathematical induction prove that $5 + 10 + 15 + \cdots + 5n = \frac{5n\,(n+1)}{2}$ **3**

(b) Let A and B be the n x n matrices and I be the identity matrix of order n x n. **4**

Check the validity of the following statements and give justification:

(i) $\exists B\ \forall A \quad A + B = I$

(ii) $\exists B\ \forall A \quad A + B = A$

(c) Let f: $\beta^2 \rightarrow \beta$be a function defined as f(0, 0) = 1, f (0, 1) = 0, f(1, 0) = 0 and f(1, 1) = 1.

Find the Boolean expression specifying the function f. **3**

(d) Let f be a permutation function defined as follows: f(1) = 2, f(2) = 4, f(3) = 1, f(4) = 3

Find the inverse of f i.e., f^{-1}. **2**

(e) Make a table to recursively calculateP_n^k, where n is the total number, k is the number of partitions, using the following conditions: $7 \geq n \geq 1$ *and* $1 \leq k < 7$ **3**

(f) An urn contains 15 balls, of which eight are red and seven are black. In how many ways can 5 balls be chosen such that two are red and three are black? **3**

(g) In how many ways can 7 people be seated around a circular table? **2**

2. (a) Show that $\sim (p \rightarrow q) \rightarrow p$ is a tautology. **2**

(b) Prove: $\sim \big(\forall\ x\ P(x)\big) \equiv \exists\ x \sim P(x)$ **3**

(c) Give the direct proof of the statement "The sum of two odd integers is always even". **3**

(d) Explain the Identity Laws of Boolean algebra. **2**

3. (a) Reduce the following Boolean expressions to simpler form: **5**

(i) $X(x_1, x_2, x_3) = (x_1 \wedge x_2 \wedge x_3) \vee (x_1 \wedge x_2) \vee (x_2 \wedge x_3)$

(ii) $X(x_1, x_2, x_3) = (x_1 \wedge x_3) \vee x_3 \vee x_2$

(b) Find the Boolean expression for the following circuit: **3**

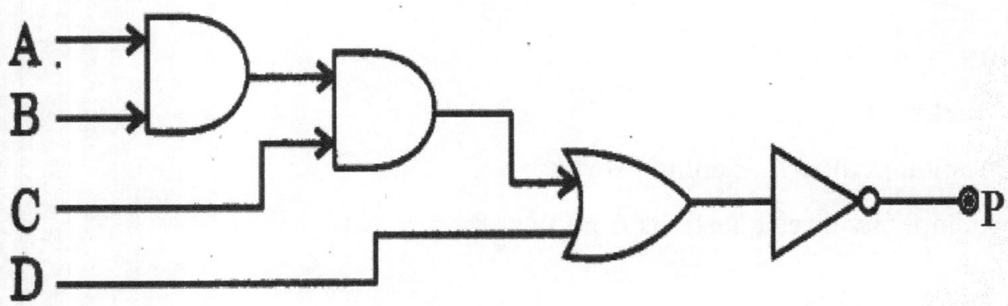

(c) Make the circuit corresponding to the following Boolean expression:

$x'_1 \vee ((x_2 \wedge x_3)' \vee (x_1 \wedge x_2 \wedge x_3))$ **2**

4. (a) Write the set expressions for the following Venn diagrams: **3**

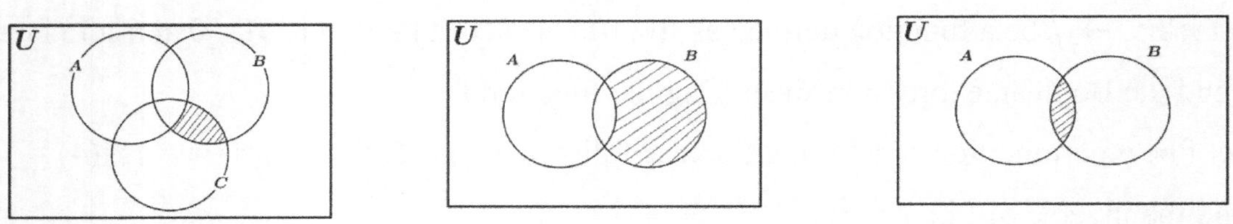

(b) What is an equivalence relation? Let A = {1, 2, 3, 4} be a set and R be an equivalence relation on A such that A/R = {{1, 2}, {3, 4}}. Write R. **3**

(c) Let f and g be the two functions such that $f(x) = x^2$ and g(x) = 2x. Define *fof, fog, gof* and *gog*. **2**

(d) Find the number of distinguishable words that can be framed from the letters of `MISSISSIPPI'. **2**

5. (a) Prove: ${}^{n+1}_{r}C = {}^{n}_{r-1}C + {}^{n}_{r}C$ **3**

(b) Use pigeonhole principle to show that if 7 colors are used to paint 50 bicycles, then at least 8 bicycles will have the same color. **2**

(c) In how many ways can 10 students be grouped into 2 groups? **3**

(d) Obtain the truth value of the disjunction of `Sun moves around the Earth' and '2 > 3'. **2**

MCS-013

MCA-Revised / BCA-Revised

Chapter 6: Term-End Examination, December- 2016

MCS-013: DISCRETE MATHEMATICS

Time: 2 hours

Maximum Marks: 50

Note: (i). Question number 1 is compulsory.

(ii). Attempt any three questions from the rest.

1. (a) Using the truth table, show that: **4**

(i). $p \leftrightarrow q \equiv (p \rightarrow q) \wedge (q \rightarrow p)$

(ii). $\sim(p \rightarrow q) \equiv p \wedge \sim q)$

(b) Show that $\sqrt{2}$ is irrational. **3**

(c) Find the Boolean expression for the output of the following circuit: **3**

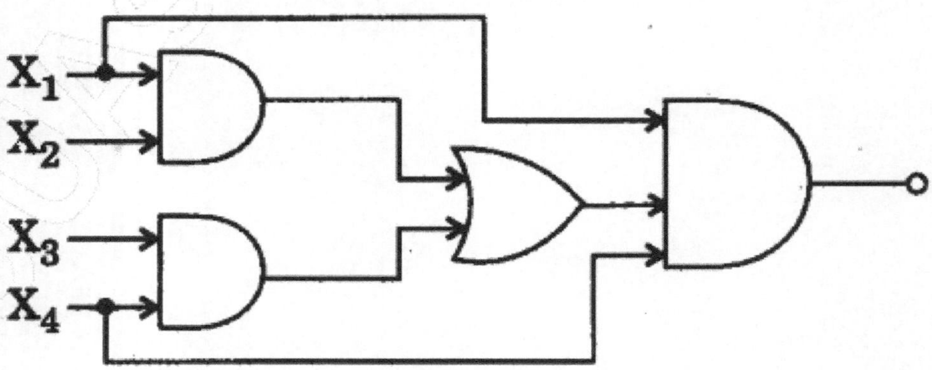

(d) Make Venn diagram for the following set of expressions: **2**

(i) $\bar{A}$

(ii) A Δ B (Symmetric difference)

(i) $A \cap B \cap C$

(ii) $A \cup B - C$

(e) Let there be a relation f defined as f = ((a, 1), (a, 2) (d, 3), (c, 4)). Is f a function?

If not, why? **2**

(f) How many distinct three-letter words can be formed from the letters of the word MAST? **2**

(g) In how many ways can a student choose 8 questions out of 10 in an exam? **2**

(h) A coin is tossed n times. What is the probability of getting exactly r heads? **2**

2. (a) Prove the following: **3**

$$(\forall\ x \sim(P(x))) \equiv \sim(\exists\ x\ P(x))$$

(b) Use Mathematical induction to prove that $1^2 + 2^2 + 3^2 + \ldots + n^2 = \frac{n(n+1)(2n+1)}{6}$ **3**

(c) Write the contrapositive and converse of the following sentence: "If 2 + 2 = 5, then I am Prime Minister of India." **2**

(d) Explain proof by contradiction, with the help of an example. **2**

3. (a) Reduce the following equations to simpler form: **4**

(i) F(a, b, c) = (a' ∧ b' ∧ c') V (a' ∧ b' ∧c) V (a ∧ b ∧ c')

(ii) F(a, b) = (a' ∧ b') V (a' ∧ b) V (a ∧ b')

(b) Construct logic circuits for the following Boolean expressions: **4**

(i) (a∧ b∧ c)V(b∧ c)'V(a∧ b)'

(ii) (a' ∧ b') V (b' ∧ c) V d

(c) What is dual of a Boolean expression? Explain the principle of duality with the help of an example. **2**

4. (a) Describe the following region using intersection and union: **2**

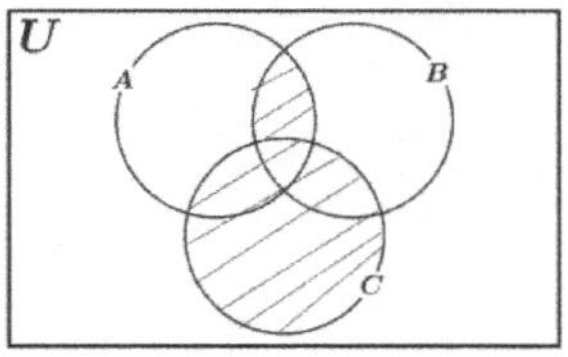

(b) Let A = {1, 2, 3, 4} be a set and a relation R is defined on A such that aRb if a ≥ b. Check if R is

(i) reflexive, (ii) symmetric, (iii) transitive, and (iv) asymmetric. **4**

(c) Let there be a function $f: A \rightarrow B$, where A and B are set defined as follows:

A={a,b,c,d},B={p,q,r,s} f= {(a, p), (b, q), (c, r), (d, p)} Explain if f is

(i) one to one, (ii) onto, (iii) bijective. **2**

(d) Prove that $A - (A - B) = A \cap B$ using Venn Diagram. **2**

5. (a) Make Pascal's triangle up to n = 6. **3**

(b) Let A and B be two mutually exclusive events such that p(A) = 0.6 and p(B) = 0-3.

What is the probability that

(i) A does not occur? (ii) A and B both occur simultaneously? **2**

(c) How many ways are there to distribute r distinct objects into 5 distinct boxes with no empty box? **3**

(d) Disprove the following statement: $(\forall\, a \in R)(\forall\, b \in R)\ [(a^2 = b^2) \Rightarrow (a = b)]$ **2**

MCS-013

MCA-Revised / BCA-Revised

Chapter 7: Term-End Examination, June- 2017

MCS-013: DISCRETE MATHEMATICS

Time: 2 hours

Maximum Marks: 50

Note: (i). Question number 1 is compulsory.

(ii). Attempt any three questions from the rest.

1. (a) Negate the following: **4**

(i) $(\forall x \exists y)\ (P(x)\ V\ Q(y))$

(ii) $(\forall x \forall y)\ (P(x) \wedge\ Q(y))$

(b) Write the contrapositive, converse and inverse of the conditional statement **2**

"The home team wins whenever it is raining."

(c) Prove that if $x^2 - 4 = 0$, then x ≠ 0 by contradiction method. **3**

(d) Draw Venn Diagram to show the following set operations: **3**

(i) $\overline{A \cup B}$

(ii) $A \subset B$

(iii) $(AUB)\ \cap C$

(e) A box contains 10 chocolates. Find the number of n ordered samples of **4**

(i) size 3 with replacement, and

(ii) size 3 without replacement.

(f) How many solutions does $x_1 + x_2 + x_3 = 11$ have where $x_1, x_2, x_3$are non-negative integers with $x_1 \leq 3, x_2 \leq 4, x_3 \leq 6$? **4**

2. (a) Two dice, one red and one white are rolled. What is the probability that the white dice turns up a smaller number than the red dice? **3**

(b) Four boys picked up 30 mangoes. In how many ways can they divide them if all the Mangoes be identical? **2**

(c) Find the Boolean expression for the following circuit: **3**

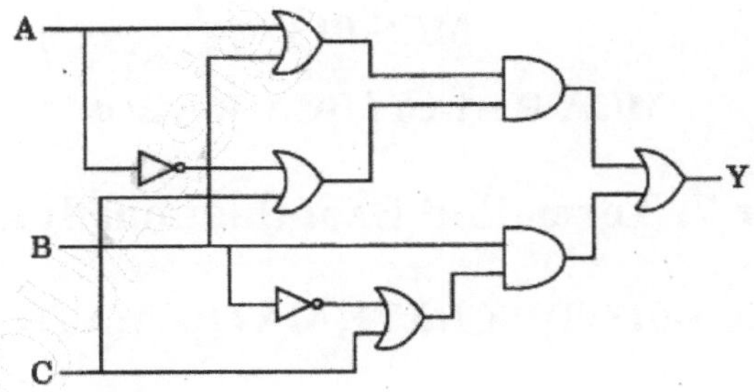

(d) How many words of three distinct letters can be formed from the letters of the word LAND? **2**

3. (a) Find the composition of the following two permutations and show that it is not commutative: $f = \begin{pmatrix} 1 & 2 & 3 & 4 \\ 2 & 1 & 4 & 3 \end{pmatrix}$ $g = \begin{pmatrix} 1 & 2 & 3 & 4 \\ 3 & 2 & 1 & 4 \end{pmatrix}$ **2**

(b) Given S = {1, 2, ..., 10} and a relation R on S where R = {(x, y) | x + y = 10}. **3**

Find whether R has the following properties or not?

(i) Reflexive (ii) Transitive (iii) Symmetric

(c) Show that the functions $f(x) = x^3$ and $g(x) = x^{1/3}$ for all $x \in R$ are inverse of each other. **3**

(d) Under what conditions on sets A and B is AxB=BxA? **3**

4. (a) Find DNF of $\sim (pVq) \leftrightarrow (pVq)$. **4**

(b) How many five-digit numbers are even? How many five-digit numbers are composed of only odd digits? **3**

(c) Draw the circuit for the following Boolean expression: $Y = AB'C + AC' + B'C$, using logic gates. **3**

5. (a) Construct truth table to check whether the following is a tautology or a contingency or a contradiction: **4**

(i) $(p \wedge q) \rightarrow (pVq)$ (ii) $((\sim q \wedge p) \wedge q)$

(b) If the temperature is - 6°, then it is cold. Write the **2**

(i) converse, and (ii) contrapositive.

(c) Show that $\frac{1}{1.2} + \frac{1}{2.3} + \ldots + \frac{1}{n.(n+1)} = \frac{n}{n+1}$ by mathematical induction. **4**

MCS-013

MCA-Revised / BCA-Revised

Chapter 8: Term-End Examination, December- 2017

MCS-013: DISCRETE MATHEMATICS

Time: 2 hours

Maximum Marks: 50

Note: (i). Question number 1 is compulsory.

(ii). Attempt any three questions from the rest.

1. (a) Translate the statement "The sum of two positive integers is positive" into a logical expression. **2**

(b) Write the negation of "If x is an integer then x is a rational number." **2**

(c) Prove that if x^2 is an even integer, then x is an even integer by contraposition method. **3**

(d) Draw a Venn Diagram to show the following set operations: **3**

(i) $A - B$

(ii) $(A \cap B)\ UC$

(iii) $(A \cap B)\ \cap C$

(e) A box contains 5 balls. Find the number of ordered samples of size 2 **4**

(i) with replacement, and

(ii) without replacement.

(f) Check whether the function f(x) = x + 1 is one-one or not. **2**

(g) How many numbers from 0 to 999 are not divisible by either 5 or 7? **4**

2. (a) A and B are mutually exclusive events such that P(A) = 0.3 and P(B) = 0.4.What is the probability that either A or B does not occur? **3**

(b) How many six-digit numbers contain exactly three different digits? **2**

(c) In how many ways can an employer distribute 100 one-rupee notes among 6 employees so that each gets at least one note? **3**

(d) How many words can be formed from A, B,C, using the letter A thrice, the letter B twice and the letter C once? **2**

3. (a) Explain Pascal's Triangle. **2**

(b) Given A = (1, 2, 3, 4) and Relation R as$\{(1, 1), (1, 2), (2, 1), (2, 2), (3, 3), (4, 4)\}$.

Examine whether R is

(i) Symmetric

(ii) Reflexive

(iii) Transitive

(c) If f: R --> R is a function such that f(x) = 3x - 4, Also, find f^{-1} **3**

(d) Let A = {a, b, c, d}, B = {1, 2, 3}, R = {(a, 2), (b, 1), (c, 2), (d, 1)}. Is R a function?

Why? **2**

4. (a) Find CNF of $\sim (p \; V \; q) \; \leftrightarrow \; (p \wedge q)$. **4**

(b) What is a proper subset? Write the number of proper subsets of the set {a, b, c, d}. **3**

(c) Draw the circuit for the following Boolean expression using logic gates

$Y = ABC + A'BC' + ABC'$. **3**

5. (a) Construct a truth table to check whether the following is a tautology or a contingency or a contradiction: **4**

(i)$p \rightarrow (q \rightarrow p)$

(ii) $p \wedge (q \wedge \sim p)$

(b) 'If today is a holiday then I will go for a movie.' Write

(i) Inverse (ii) Contrapositive **2**

(c) Show that$n^2 > 2n + 1$ for n ≥ 3 by Mathematical Induction. **4**

MCS-013

MCA-Revised / BCA-Revised

Chapter 9: Term-End Examination, June- 2018

MCS-013: DISCRETE MATHEMATICS

Time: 2 hours

Maximum Marks: 50

Note: (i). Question number 1 is compulsory.

(ii). Attempt any three questions from the rest.

1. (a) How many three digit numbers are there with no digit repeated? **2**

(b) Show that $\sim (pVq) = \sim p \wedge \sim q$ **2**

(c) Prove that $ab + [c\,(a' + b')] = ab + c$ **3**

(d) Find the domain for which the function $f(x) = 3x^2 - 1$ and $g(x) = 1 - 5x$ are equal. Also find a domain for which the functions are not equal. **4**

(e) Prove that (A— B)U B = A U B **3**

(f) If there are 12 persons in a party, and if each two of them shake hands with each other, how many handshakes happen in the party? **3**

(g) Show that for integers greater than zero:

$2^n >= n + 1$ **3**

2. (a) Use Mathematical induction to prove that

$$1^2 + 2^2 + 3^2 + \ldots + n^2 = \frac{n(n+1)(2n+1)}{6}$$ **4**

(b) Draw Venn diagrams to represent the following for sets A, B and C. **4**

(i) $A\Delta B$ (ii) $A \cap B \cup C$

(c) Find n if 2P(n, 2) + 50 = P(2n, 2). **2**

3. (a) If f: R --> R is a function such that f(x) = 3x + 5, prove that f is one-one onto. **4**

(b) Show that $pV\ (q \wedge r) \leftrightarrow (pVq) \wedge (pVr)$ is a tautology. **3**

(c) Find in how many ways can 25 identical books be placed in 5 identical boxes. **3**

4. (a) Find the Boolean Expression for the given circuit. **3**

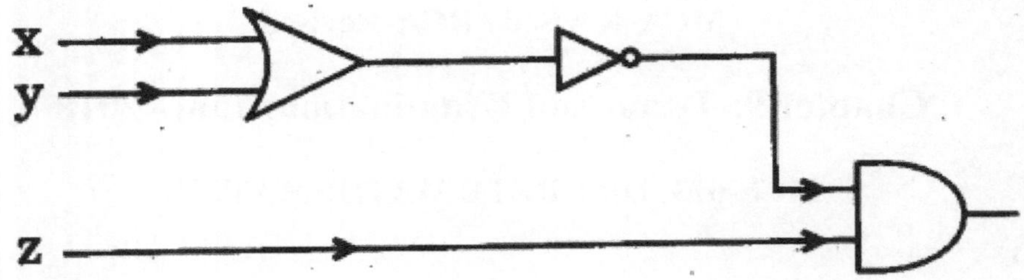

(b) Show whether $\sqrt{17}$ is rational or irrational. **4**

(c) Prove that $p \leftrightarrow q \equiv (p \Rightarrow q) \wedge (q \Rightarrow p)$

5. (a) Let A = {a, b, c, d}, B = (1, 2, 3} and R = {(a, 2), (b, 1), (c, 2), (d, 1)}. Is R a function? Why? **2**

(b) How many permutations are there of the letters, taken all at a time, of the word DISTINCT? **3**

(c) Show that in any group of 30 people, we can always find 5 people who were born on the same day of the week. **3**

(d) Find how many 4-digit numbers are odd **2**

MCS-013

MCA-Revised / BCA-Revised

Chapter 10: Term-End Examination, December- 2018

MCS-013: DISCRETE MATHEMATICS

Time: 2 hours

Maximum Marks: 50

Note: (i). Question number 1 is compulsory.

(ii). Attempt any three questions from the rest.

1. (a) Find the dual of

(i) $A \cap (B \cap C) = (A \cap B) \cap C$and (ii) $(A \, U \, B) \cap (A \, U \, C)$. **4**

(b) Give the geometric representation of R x {2}. R is the set of Real Numbers. **4**

(c) Find the number of distinct sets of 5 cards that can be dealt from a deck of 52 cards. **4**

(d) Find the number of ways of placing n people in (n - 1) rooms, no room being empty. **4**

(e) Verify that $p \wedge q \wedge (\sim p)$ is a contradiction and $p \rightarrow q \leftrightarrow \sim p \, V q$ is a tautology. **4**

2. (a) Prove that if $x, y \in I$ such that xy is odd, then both x and y are odd, by proving its contrapositive. I is the set of Integers. **5**

(b) Design a logic circuit to operate a light bulb by two switchesx_1 and x_2. **5**

3. (a) A box contains 3 red, 3 blue and 4 white socks. In how many ways can 8 socks be pulled out of the box, one at a time, if order is important? **5**

(b) Suppose 5 points are chosen at random within or on the boundary of an equilateral triangle of side 1 metre. Show how we can find two points at a distance of at most $\frac{1}{2}$ metre. **5**

4. (a) Find the boolean expression for the following circuit: **4**

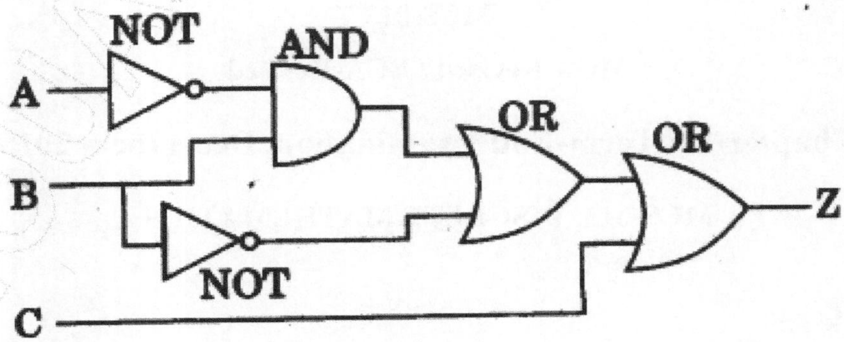

(b) Find the inverse of the following function: $f(x) .= x^3 — 3$ **3**

(c) State and explain Pigenhole principle. **3**

5. (a) A car manufacturer has 5 service centres in a city. 10 identical cars were served in these centres for a particular mechanical defect. In how many ways could the cars have been distributed at the various centres? **6**

(b) Show that $\sqrt{5}$ is irrational **4**

MCS-013

MCA-Revised / BCA-Revised

Chapter 11: Term-End Examination, June- 2019

MCS-013: DISCRETE MATHEMATICS

Time: 2 hours

Maximum Marks: 50

Note: (i). Question number 1 is compulsory.

(ii). Attempt any three questions from the rest.

1. (a) Obtain the truth value of the disjunction of "The earth is flat" and "3 + 5 = 2." **4**

(b) Write down the truth table of $(p \rightarrow q \wedge -r) \leftrightarrow (r\ q)$. **4**

(c) Show that $2^n > n^3$ for$n \geq 10$. **4**

(d) Design a logic circuit capable of operating a central light bulb in a hall by three switches x_1, x_2, x_3(say) placed at the three entrances to that hall. **4**

(e) If X ={a, b, c} and Y = (1,2, 3) , find$X \times X$ *and* $X \times Y$ **4**

2. (a) Suppose 10 people have exactly the same briefcase, which they leave at a counter. The briefcases are handed back to the people randomly. What is the probability that no one gets the right briefcase? **5**

(b) What is a function? Explain the following types of functions with example: **5**

(i) Bijective

(ii) Surjective

3. (a) Show that: 5 $(p \rightarrow \sim q) \wedge (p \rightarrow -r) \equiv \sim [p \wedge (q\ V\ r)]$. **5**

(b) Prove that $(x\ V\ y)' = x' \wedge y'$ and$(x \wedge y)' = x'\ V\ y'$ **5**

4. (a)Let f: $\beta^2 \rightarrow \beta$be a function defined as **5**

f(0, 0) = 1, f (0, 1) = 1,

f(1, 0) = 0 and f(1, 1) = 1.

Find the Boolean expression 'specifying the function f

(b) Give the expression $(x_1' \, V \, (x_2x_3)) \, \wedge \, (x_2 \, V \, x'_4)$, find the corresponding circuit, where x_i $(1 \leq i \leq 4)$are assumed to be inputs to the circuitary. **5**

5. (a) There is a village that consists of two types of people-those who always tell the truth and those who always lie. Suppose that you visit the village and two villagers A and B come up to you.Further suppose: A says, "B always tells the truth" and B says, "A and I are of opposite types."What types are A and B? **5**

(b) Draw a Venn diagram to represent the following: **5**

(i) $(A \cup B) \cap (A \sim C)$

(ii) $(A \cup B) \cap C$

MCS-013

MCA-Revised / BCA-Revised

Chapter 12: Term-End Examination, December- 2019

MCS-013: DISCRETE MATHEMATICS

Time: 2 hours

Maximum Marks: 50

Note: (i). Question number 1 is compulsory.

(ii). Attempt any three questions from the rest.

1. (a) Construct the truth table for the formula:

$\alpha = (P \rightarrow (Q \rightarrow R) \rightarrow ((P \rightarrow Q) \rightarrow (P \rightarrow R))$ Check whether it is a tautology or not. **5**

(b) Show that$\sqrt{2}$ is irrational. **4**

(c) Given A = {1, 3, 5, 7), B = {2, 3, 5, 8). List all the elements of $(A \cap B) \times (B - A)$. **3**

(d) Show that the function $f\ (x) = x^3$ and $g\ (x) = x^{1/3}$ for all x e R are inverse of one another. **2**

(e) Give the direct proof of the statement: 3 "The product of two odd integers is odd." **3**

(f) How many license plate containing two letter followed by three digit can be formed 2 If the letters as well as digits can be repeated. **3**

2. (a) Find the power set of: **2**

A= (a, b, c, d}.

(b) In a group of students, 70 have a personal computer, 120 have a personal stereo and 41 have both.How many own at least one of these device? Draw an appropriate Venn diagram. **4**

(c) ${}^{1000}_{98}C = {}^{999}_{97}C + {}_{901}^{x}C$Find x. **4**

3. (a) Draw logical circuit for the following logical expression: **3**

$x_1 \wedge x'_2$

(b) Find the probability of getting the sum 9 or 11 in a single throw of two dice. **3**

(c) A drawer contains ten black and ten white socks. What ie the least no. of socks one must pull out to be sure to get a matched pair? **4**

4. (a) A problem of discrete mathematics is given to three students whose chances of solving $\frac{1}{2}, \frac{1}{3}$ *and* $\frac{1}{4}$What is the probability that exactly one of them solves it? **3**

   (b) A house has 4 doors and 10 windows. In how many ways can a thief rob the house by entering through a window and exiting through a door? **3**

   (c) A committee of 2 hawkers and 3 shopkeepers is to formed from 7 hawkers and 10 shopkeepers. Find the no. of ways in which this can be done if a particular shopkeeper is included and a particular hawker is excluded. **4**

5. (a) Show that 5 divides $n^5 - n$, where It is a non-negative integer. **4**

   (b) Write the negation of the following statement: **2**

   "If he studies he will pass the examination."

   (c) Give the output of the given circuit: **4**

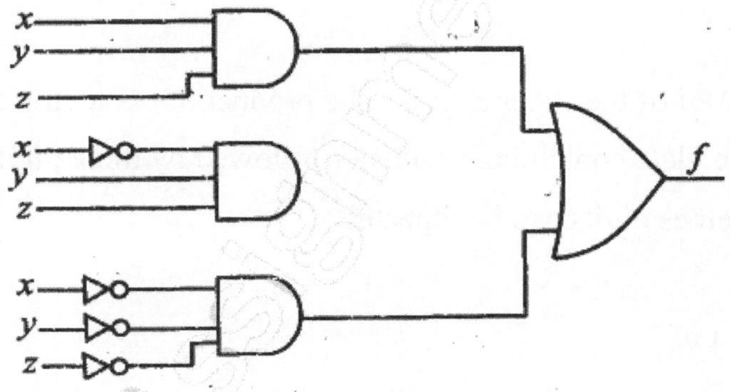

MCS-013

MCA-Revised / BCA-Revised

Chapter 13: Term-End Examination, June- 2020

MCS-013: DISCRETE MATHEMATICS

Time: 2 hours

Maximum Marks: 50

Note: (i). Question number 1 is compulsory.

(ii). Attempt any three questions from the rest.

1. (a) Check whether the following formula is tautology, contradiction or contingency: **5**

$$\sim ((P \rightarrow Q) \rightarrow ((R \vee P) \rightarrow (R \vee Q)))$$

(b) Two finite sets have x and y number of elements. The total number of subsets of the first set is four times the total number of subsets of second set. Find out the value of $x - y$. **4**

(c) In a group of 400 people 250 can speak in English only and 70 can speak Hindi only.3

(i) How many can speak English?

(ii) How many can speak Hindi?

(iii) How many can speak both English and Hindi?

(d) If f: A → B and g: B → C are injective function, then gof: A → C is an injective function. Prove or disprove. **3**

(e) Use the method of proof by contradiction to show that x e R. if $x^3 + 4x = 0$, then x = 0. **3**

(f) Three persons enter in a railway compartment. If there are 5 seats vacant, in how many Ways they can take these seats? **2**

2. (a) Given: A = {1, 3, 5, 7} B = {2, 3, 5, 8}

List the elements of $(A \times B) \times (B - A)$. Is $(A \times B)\ (B - A)$ a subset of A x B? **5**

(b) Prove that: ${}^{n}_{r}C + {}_{r-1}^{\ \ n}C = {}^{n+1}_{\ \ r}C\ (0 \leq r \leq n)$ **5**

3. (a) Show that in any set of eleven integers there are two which are divisible by 10,

by applying pigeonhole principle. **3**

(b) How many solutions are there of: **4**

$x + y + z = 17$ subject to the constraints: $x \geq 1$, $y \geq 2$, $z \geq 3$

(c) if: $P(A) = \frac{1}{4}$, $P(B) = \frac{2}{5}$ and $P(A \cup B) = \frac{1}{2}$

Find: (i) $P(A \cap B)$ (ii) $P(A \cap B')$

4. (a) Five balls are drawn from a bag containing 6 white and 4 black balls. What is the probability that 3 are white and 2 black? **3**

(b) From the digit 1, 2, 3, 4, 5, 6, how many three digit odd numbers can be formed when

(i) repetition of digit is allowed? **2**

(ii) repetition of digit is not allowed? **2**

(c) How many numbers divisible by 2 lying between 50,000 and 70,000 can be formed from the digits 3, 4, 5, 6, 7, 8, 9, no digit being repeated in any number. **3**

5. (a) Show that: $1.2 + 2.3 + \cdots \ldots \ldots \ldots \ldots .. \; n(n+1) = \frac{n(n+1)(n+2)}{3}$ **4**

(b) Write the negation of the following statement: **2**

If it is raining, then the game is cancelled.

(c) Draw the circuit represented by the following Boolean function: **4**

$$f : xy + \overline{xy}$$

MCS-013

MCA-Revised / BCA-Revised

Chapter 14: Term-End Examination, February- 2021

MCS-013: DISCRETE MATHEMATICS

Time: 2 hours

Maximum Marks: 50

Note: (i). Question number 1 is compulsory.

(ii). Attempt any three questions from the rest.

1. (a) Show using truth table whether $(p \cup q \cup r)$ *and* $(p \vee r) \cup (q \vee r)$ are equivalent or not. **3**

(b) Using Mathematical Induction, prove that: $1 + 2 + 3 + \cdots + n = \frac{n(n+1)}{2}$ **4**

(c) Prove that if A is a set with n elements, then $|P(A)| = 2^n$. **3**

(d) If there are 7 men and 5 women, how many circular arrangements are possible in which women do not sit adjacent to each other? **3**

(e) Find Boolean expression for the following logic circuit: **3**

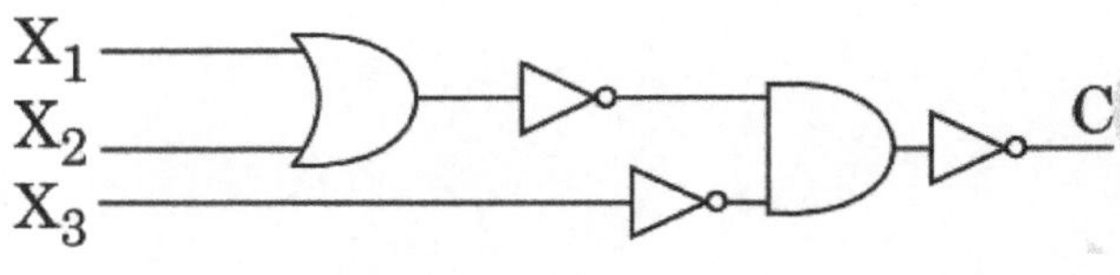

(f) If f : R□R be a function given by $f(x) = x^3 - 2$, find whether f^{-1} exists or not. If f^{-1} exists, find it. **4**

2. (a) How many words can be formed using the letters of the word "DEPARTMENT", if each letter must be used at most once? **4**

(b) Give geometric representation for {1, 3}□ {−2, 3}. **2**

(c) Show that $(p \rightarrow q) \rightarrow q = p \vee q$ **2**

(d) Find the number of ways to distribute 20 distinct objects into 10 distinct boxes with at least 4 boxes remaining empty. **2**

3. (a) Draw Venn diagrams for the following expressions: **3**

(i) A□B□C (ii) A □B□C (iii) A □B□ C

(b) Draw logic circuit for the following Boolean expression: **2**

$(X_1 \cup X'_2)$ Ú$(X'_1 \cup X'_2)$

(c) Write the following statements in the symbolic form: **2**

(i) Every thing is correct.

(ii) All birds can not fly.

(d) Explain Principle of Duality with the help of an example. **3**

4. (a) Show that $\sqrt{11}$ is irrational. **4**

(b)What is an indirect proof? Explain with the help of an example. **3**

(c) Explain De Morgan's Laws with the help of Venn diagram. **3**

5. (a) In a ten-question true-false exam, a student must achieve five correct answers to pass. If he selects his answers randomly, what is the probability that he will pass? **3**

(b) In how many ways can an employer distribute 50 twenty-rupee notes among 5 employees so that each gets at least one note? **2**

(c) Show that in any group of 30 people, you can always find 5 people who were born on the same day of the week. **3**

(d) Draw truth table for: **2**

(p□ q) □p

MCS-013

MCA-Revised / BCA-Revised

Chapter 15: Term-End Examination, June- 2021

MCS-013: DISCRETE MATHEMATICS

Time: 2 hours

Maximum Marks: 50

Note: (i). Question number 1 is compulsory.

(ii). Attempt any three questions from the rest.

1. (a) Write the truth value of the conjunction of: ''The earth is round'' and ''3 > 4''. **2**

(b) Use Mathematical Induction to prove that: **4**

$1 + \frac{1}{4} + \frac{1}{9} + \ldots \frac{1}{n^2} \leq 2 - \frac{1}{n}$ 2 -£ n " n ∩ N

(c) If f: R□R is a function such that f(x) = 3x – 2, prove that f is injective. Also find the inverse of f. **5**

(d)Show that $p \cup (q \cap r)$ and $(p \cup q) \cup (p \cup r)$ are logically equivalent. **3**

(e) A and B are two mutually exclusive events such that P(A) = 0.4 and P(B) = 0.2. **3**

What is the probability that:

(i) A does not occur?

(ii) A or B does not occur?

(iii) Either A or B does not occur?

(f) Find the number of ways of placing n people in n – 1 rooms, no room being empty. **3**

2. (a) What is integer partition? Write down all the partitions of 8. Also find P_8^4 and P_8^7. **4**

(b) Find Boolean Expression for the following logical circuit: **4**

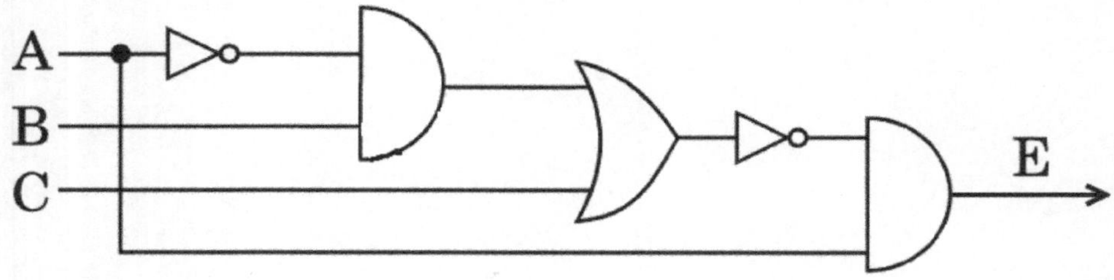

(c) Let two functions be such that $f(x) = x^2 + 2$ and $g(x) = 2x$. Define *fog* and *gof*. **2**

3. (a) Reduce the following Boolean Expression to simpler form: **4**

$E(X_1, X_2, X_3) = (X_1 \cup X_2 \cup X_3)(X_1 \cap X_2) \cup (X_2 \cap X_3)$.

(b) Show that $\sim (p \to q) \to p$is a tautology **2**

(c) Prove that $\sqrt{2}$ is irrational. **4**

4. (a) What is Relation? How is relation different from function? Explain any two properties of relations with an example. **5**

(b) A company has the following professionals: Project Leaders – 5, Team Leaders – 6, System Architects – 3.Find how many different committees can be formed of 10 professionals,each containing at least 2 Project Leaders, at least 3 Team Leaders and at least 1 System Architect. **3**

(c) Find the dual of A□ B □C **2**

5. (a) Explain the Identity Laws of Boolean Algebra. **2**

(b) State and prove the Addition Theorem of Probability. **4**

(c) Verify that$p \cup q \cup \sim p$ is a contradiction. **2**

(d) What is Exclusive Disjunction? Write truth table for p □q **2**

MCS-013

MCA-Revised / BCA-Revised

Chapter 16: Term-End Examination, December- 2021

MCS-013: DISCRETE MATHEMATICS

Time: 2 hours

Maximum Marks: 50

Note: (i). Question number 1 is compulsory.

(ii). Attempt any three questions from the rest.

1. (a) Explain if the following sentences are proposition or not and why: **4**

(i) Sun rises in the east.

(ii) Prepare for your exam.

(iii) Raju is 10-year old.

(iv) How far is Mumbai from here? (b) Prove that:

$$1 + 2 + 3 + \cdots + n = \frac{n(n+1)}{2}$$ using Mathematical induction **4**

(c) What is a proper subset? Explain with the help of a suitable example. **2**

(d) Find number of integers between 100 and 999 consisting of distinct even digits. **2**

(e) If $f(x) = x^3$ and $g(x) = (x^2 + 1)$□ x □R, where R is the set of real numbers **3**

Find: (i) (f o g), (ii) (g o f), (iii) (g o g)

(f) Find the number of distinguishable words that can be framed from the letters of the word **"UNIVERSITY"**. **2**

(g) Find dual of (A □B) □C and (A□ B) □ C **3**

2. (a) Show that $\sqrt{17}$ is irrational. **4**

(b) Find the Boolean expression for the following logic circuit: **4**

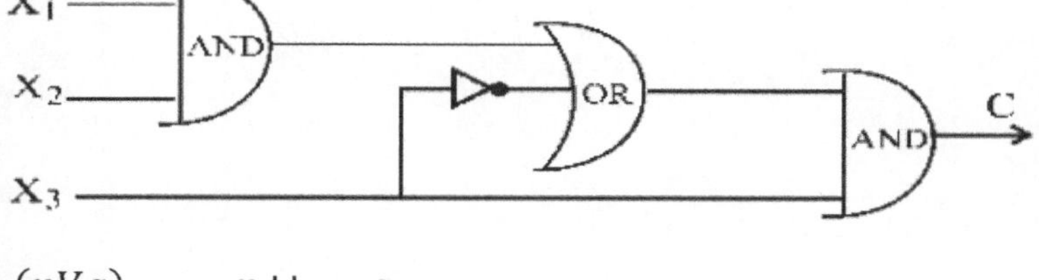

(c) Show that: $\sim(pVq) = \sim p \cup \sim q$ **2**

3. (a) Write the set expressions for the following Venn diagrams:

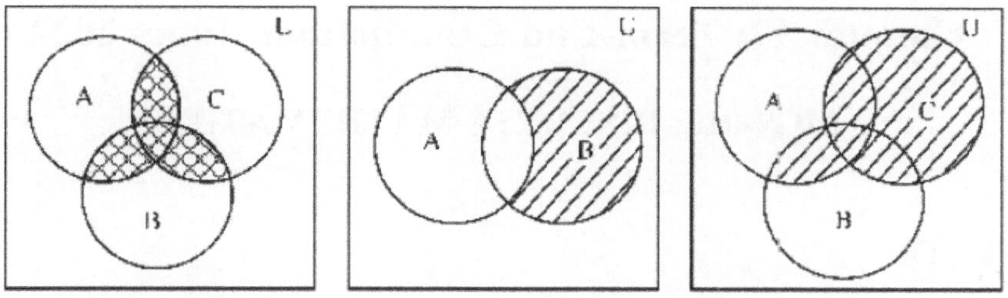

(b) Prove that: ${}^{n}_{r}C + {}_{r-1}^{n}C = {}^{n+1}_{r}C \ (0 \le r \le n)$ 3

(c) A die is rolled once. Find the probability of each of the following events: 4

(i) getting an odd number

(ii) getting at most 3

(iii) getting at least 3

(iv) getting at least 7

4. (a) Make truth table for the following: 2

$p \rightarrow (\sim q \, V \sim r) \cup (p \, V \sim r)$

(b) Give geometric representation for the following: 2

R × {4}; where R is a natural number.

(c) What is Relation? Explain equivalence relation with the help of an example. 4

(d) State and explain Pigeonhole principle. 2

5. (a) Draw logic circuit for the following Boolean expression: 4

(X' + Y + Z) + (X + Y + Z') + (X'.Y)

(b) In how many ways 10 students can be grouped into 3 groups? 3

(c) What is power set? Find power set of set A = {1, 2, 4, 6}. 3

MCS-013

MCA-Revised / BCA-Revised

Chapter 17: Term-End Examination, June- 2022

MCS-013: DISCRETE MATHEMATICS

Time: 2 hours

Maximum Marks: 50

Note: (i). Question number 1 is compulsory.

(ii). Attempt any three questions from the rest.

1. (a) Use pigeonhole principles to find the minimum number of cars that will have same color; if 20 cars are painted using 6 colors. **2**

(b) Show that $\sqrt{3}$ is irrational. **4**

(c) Draw the logic circuit for the following Boolean expression: **4**

$$(X_1 \cup X_2 \cup X'_3) \cap (X'_1 \cap X'_2 \cup X_3)$$

(d) Write the set expression (shaded part) for the following Venn diagrams:

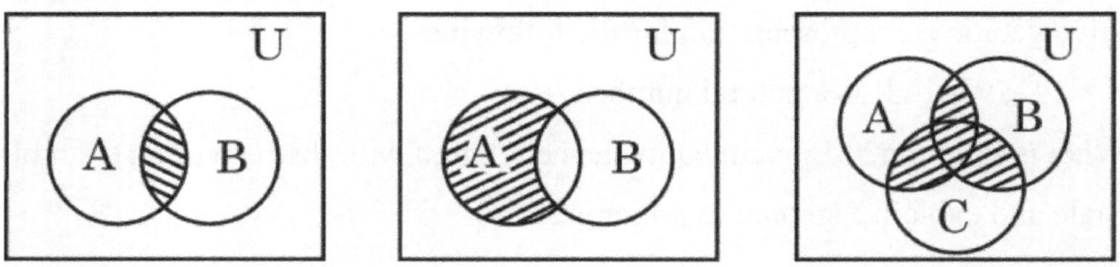

(e) Write suitable mathematical statement that can be represented by(" x)(" y)($ z)P **2**

(f) Disprove that (a ∩ R)(b ∩ R) [(a^2 = b^2)Þ(a = b)] using a counter-example. **2**

(g) There are 5 women and 6 men. A committee has to be formed of 3 people. In how many ways can this be done if at least one woman should be there in the committee? **3**

2. (a) Prove using mathematical induction that ⟦(1+x)⟧ ^n>1+nxfor all x > 0 and n > 1. **5**

(b) What is proper subset? Explain with the help of an example. **2**

(c) Show p ∪(p ∩ q) ↔p is a tautology. **3**

3. (a) Every function is a relation. Is every relation a function? Why? **3**

(b) Explain circular permutation with the help of an example. **3**

(c) Find the Boolean expression of Q in the logic circuit given below: **4**

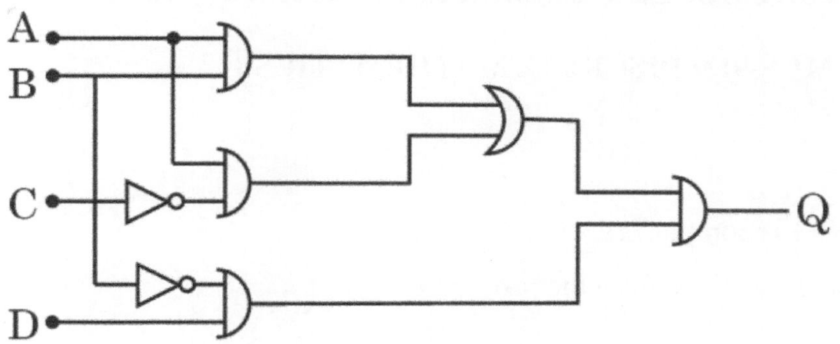

4. (a) If A and B are two mutually exclusive events such that P(A) = 0·4 and P(B) = 0·2, what is the probability that either A or B does not occur? **2**

(b) Give the geometric representation of {3} □ R **2**

(c) Present a direct proof of the statement "Square of an odd integer is odd." **3**

(d) Find the inverse of the function f(x)= (x-4)/(x-3). **3**

5. (a) Show that C(n, m) C(m, k) = C(n, k) C(n – k, m – k) for 1□ k □ m□n.

3

(b) How many 3-letter words can be formed from the letters of the word "HAPPY"? **2**

(c) What is contradiction? Show whether p ∪ q ∪~ p is a contradiction or not. **3**

(d) Draw the Venn diagram for the expression A □B □C

2

MCS-013

MCA-Revised / BCA-Revised

Chapter 18: Term-End Examination, December- 2022

MCS-013: DISCRETE MATHEMATICS

Time: 2 hours

Maximum Marks: 50

Note: (i). Question number 1 is compulsory.

(ii). Attempt any three questions from the rest.

1. (a) Write De Morgan's laws for predicate logic and propositional logic. **4**

(b) Show that $[(p \rightarrow q) \wedge \sim q] \rightarrow \sim p$ is a tautology, without using truth table. **4**

(c) Show that$2^n > n^3$ for $n \geq 10$ **4**

(d) Construct the logic circuit represented by the Boolean expression

$(X'_1 \wedge X_2) \vee (X_1 \vee X_3)$ whereX_1, X_2, $X_3$are assumed inputs to the circuit. **4**

(e) What is the difference between permutation and combination? If n couples are at a dance party,in how many ways can the men and women be pained for a single dance? **4**

2. (a) If m and n are positive integers, show that: **3**

$(m + n)! \geq m! + n!$

(b) Find inverse of the function f (x), where **3**

f(x)= x^3 - 3

(c) Show whether √15 is a rational or irrational. **4**

3. (a) Find the Boolean expression corresponding to the following circuit.

Also obtain the CNF of the expression: **4**

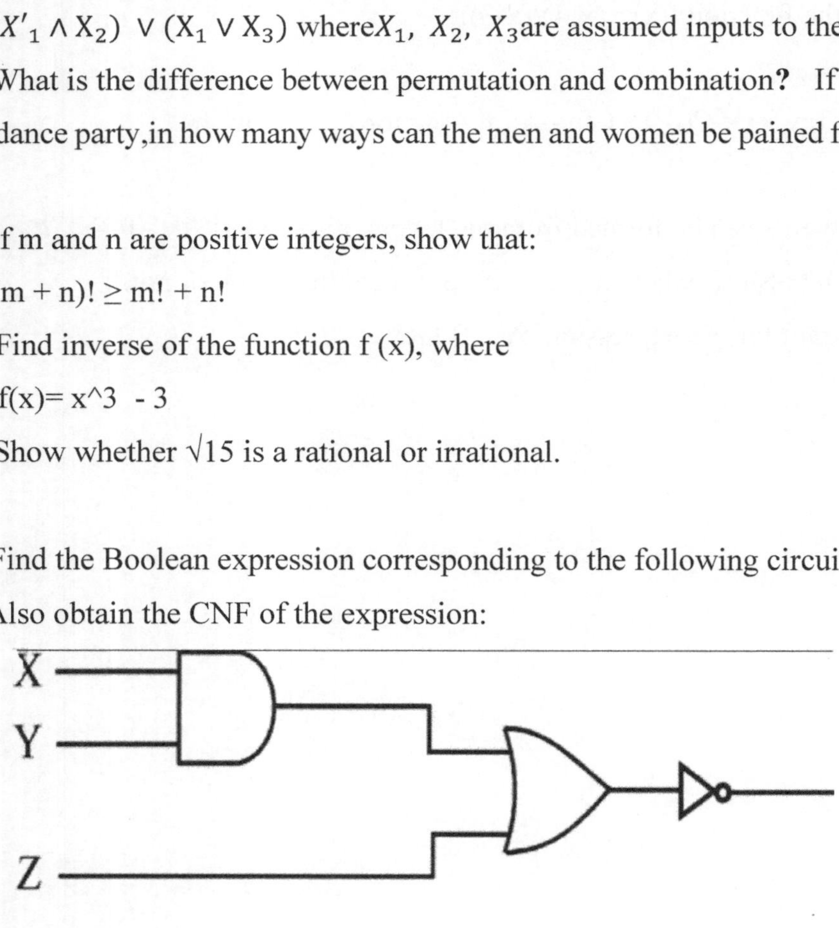

(b) What is Cartesian product? Give the geometric representation of the Cartesian product of A and B, where A = {2, 3, 4} and B = {1, 4}. **4**

(c) Let A = {a, b, c, d} and B = {1, 2, 3} and R = {(a, 2), (b, 1), (c, 2), (d, 1)}. Is R a function? Why? **2**

4. (a) What is Piegonhole principle? Explain with a suitable example. **3**

(b) Determine all the integer solution to $x_1 + x_2 + x_3 + x_4 = 9$. $where\ x_i \geq 1, i = 1, 2,3,4$. **3**

(c) Prove by induction that $n^3 - n$ is divisible by 3 for all positive integers. **4**

5. (a) If there are 5 men and 4 women, how many circular arrangements are possible in which women don't sit adjacent to each other? **4**

(b) Write the principle of duality. Find the dual of: **6**

(i) $\sim(X \wedge Y) \vee Z$ (ii) $(X \vee Y) \vee (X \vee Z)$

MCS-013

MCA-Revised / BCA-Revised

Chapter 19: Term-End Examination, December- 2023

MCS-013: DISCRETE MATHEMATICS

Time: 2 hours

Maximum Marks: 50

Note: (i). Question number 1 is compulsory.

(ii). Attempt any three questions from the rest.

1. (a) Using the truth table, show that: p « q ≡ (p ® q) ∪ (q® p) **2**

(b) Prove that $\sqrt{2}$ is irrational. **2**

(c) Find the Boolean expression for the output for the following circuit: **2**

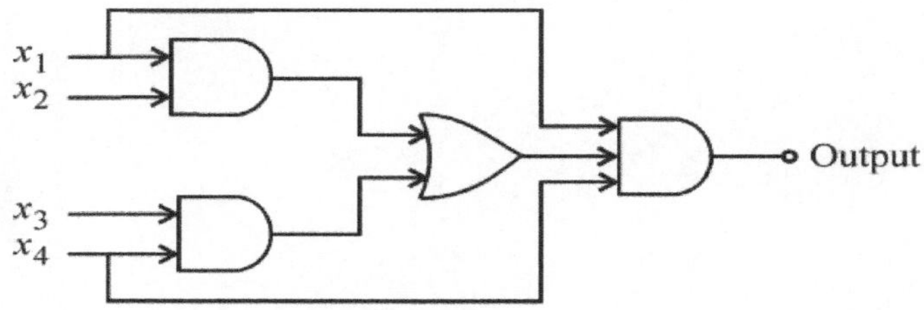

(d) Make a Venn diagram for the following set of expressions: **2**

(i) $\bar{A}$

(ii) $A \Delta B$ (Symmetric Difference)

(e) Find the domain for which the function $f(x) = 3x^2 - 1$ *and* $g(x) = 1 - 5x$are equal. **2**

(f) In how many ways can a student choose 8 questions out of 10 questions in an exam? **2**

(g) Prove the following: **2**

$$\sim \left(\exists_x P(x)\right) \equiv \forall_x(\sim P(x))$$

(h) Let$f(x) = \frac{1}{x}$ *and* $g(x) = x^3 + 2,$ *where* $x \in R$ Find $(f + g)(x)$ *and* $(fg)(x)$. **2**

(i) Use Mathematical induction to prove that $1^2 + 2^2 + 3^2 + \ldots + n^2 = \frac{n(n+1)(2n+1)}{6}$ **4**

(j) How many distinct three-letter words can be formed from the letters of the word "MUST"? **2**

2. (a) Let A = R – {3} and B = R – {1}: f: A □ B, defined by $f(x) = \frac{x-2}{x-3}$ Find f^{-1}. **5**

(b) Write the contrapositive and converse of the following statement: **2**

"if 2 + 2 = 5, then I am a Lion".

(c) What is dual in a Boolean expression? Explain the principle of duality with the help of an example. **3**

3. (a) Compare predicate and preposition logic. Give De Morgan's laws for both. Also, give suitable example for both. **5**

(b) Explain Pigeon hole principle with suitable example. **5**

4. (a) Let: A = □a,b,c,d□ B = {1,2,3□ and R = {(a,2), (b,1), (c,2), (d,1)}. Is R a function? Explain. **2**

(b) Show that in any group of 30 people, we can always find 5 people who were born on the same day of the week. **3**

(c) Write short notes on any two of the following: **5**

(i) Modus-Ponens

(ii) Disjunctive syllogism

(iii) Contrapositive

5. (a) Show that for integer greater than zero: **3**

$$2^n >= n + 1$$

(b) Let A and B be two mutually exclusive events such that p(A) = 0.6 and p(B) = 0.3

What is the probability that: **2**

(i) A does not occur?

(ii) A and B both occur simultaneously?

(c) Reduce the following expression to the simpler form: **2**

$$F(a,b,c) = (a' \cup b' \cup c')\text{Ú}(a' \cup b' \cup c)\text{Ú}\,(a \cup b \cup c')$$

(d) Prove that: ${}^{n}_{r}C + {}_{r-1}^{\ \ n}C = {}^{n+1}_{\ \ r}C \ (0 \leq r \leq n)$ **3**

Printed at Repro India Ltd.